What Do You Mean, "Study The Bible"?

A Survey Of The Old Testament For High School Groups

Katherine Bailey Babb

CSS Publishing Company, Inc., Lima, Ohio

WHAT DO YOU MEAN, "STUDY THE BIBLE"?

Dedicated to my wonderful
High School Sunday school students

Copyright © 2001 by
CSS Publishing Company, Inc.
Lima, Ohio

All rights reserved. No part of this publication may be reproduced in any manner whatsoever without the prior permission of the publisher, except in the case of brief quotations embodied in critical articles and reviews. Inquiries should be addressed to: Permissions, CSS Publishing Company, Inc., P.O. Box 4503, Lima, Ohio 45802-4503.

Illustrations from ClickArt Religious Graphics © 1999 TLC Multimedia Inc., Novato, California.

For more information about CSS Publishing Company resources, visit our website at www.csspub.com.

ISBN 978-0-7880-1802-2

PRINTED IN U.S.A.

Table Of Contents

Introduction: What Do You Mean, "Study The Bible"?   5

Lesson 1: Creation!   7
Genesis 1, 2

Lesson 2: Obedience?   9
Genesis 2, 3

Lesson 3: Jealousy, The Green-Eyed Monster   12
Genesis 4

Lesson 4: Through A Flood!   15
Genesis 5

Lesson 5: Precious Possessions — What Would You Give Up?   16
Genesis 12-25

Lesson 6: Hey, Joe, Nice Coat!   17
Genesis 37-45

Lesson 7: Holy Moses!   19
Exodus 1-9

Lesson 8: Laws, Laws, Laws ...   20
Leviticus, Deuteronomy

Lesson 9: Joshua Fit The Battle Of Jericho, And ...   22
Joshua

Lesson 10: Here Come The Judges!   25
Judges

Lesson 11: David, A Man After God's Own Heart — Say WHAT?   26
1 and 2 Samuel, 1 Kings

Lesson 12: Power! — The Prophet Elijah 28
    1 Kings

Lesson 13: Hey! Ain't No Way That's Fair! What's Up With THIS? 29
    Job

Lesson 14: How Are You Feeling? 30
    Psalms, Proverbs, Ecclesiastes, Song of Solomon

Lesson 15: Okay, NOW You're In Trouble! 33
    Prophets

Introduction

What Do You Mean, "Study The Bible"?

As a teacher of a high school Sunday school class, my first question to the group was, "What would you like to study this year?" Dead silence and furtive glances. Clearly, this was not a good question. It was scary!

Then one girl snorted, "I don't care. I just don't want to study the BIBLE!" Everyone around the room nodded. The Bible was a definite no-no: "too hard to understand," "too much work to read," "boring."

So that year, we didn't study the Bible. We had lessons on different religions and on different denominations. We studied cults, and we had trivia games. We did in-depth discussions about all kinds of topics, and we did do some "light" Bible study in the midst of all this.

But it became increasingly and painfully clear to me that although these teens had grown up in the church, they were woefully ignorant of even the most basic tenets of the Bible and of the faith that they professed to have. To me, the Bible is exciting! It is full of the voice of God speaking to me with challenge, with love, and with grace. I want my students to share my feelings. So, with a bit of fear and trepidation, and much, much prayer both for the process and the participants, I determined that THIS year, we were going to study the Bible and LIKE IT!

These lessons are the product of that determination. I have to tell you that, so far, I am thrilled with the results (sometimes ...). We are told in Hebrews 4:12 that "the word of God is living and active, sharper than any two-edged sword, piercing until it divides soul from spirit, joints from marrow; it is able to judge the thoughts and intentions of the heart." When my class started reading Genesis together, in a "safe" environment where it was okay to ask any questions, it was exciting. Many questions were brought up and discussed. We all left with many questions, not a lot of concrete answers, but with our heads full of the wonder of a God who created a universe! It was exciting. Later that morning, I saw one of the young people kneeling at the communion rail for a long time, and my heart overflowed. I knew that he was questioning, but he was obviously asking the right person!

If this is threatening to you as a Sunday School teacher, and you do not feel like a competent Bible scholar, that's okay! Arm yourself beforehand with Bible dictionaries, commentaries, and helps. Study up before each lesson. Ask your pastor for resources. And admit to your class that this is a quest in which you are participating, too! Don't be afraid to stretch and grow in your own beliefs, and don't be afraid to share your beliefs with them. Just avoid being "preachy" — you know what happens when you do that! Instant turn-off and dull stares.

With high school students, it is important to realize that this is an extremely difficult time in their lives. On one hand, they are at an age when, in other countries and cultures, they are already deemed adults; and they have many of the qualifications for being adults. On the other hand, they are still students, still at home with parents, still "finding out" who they are and who they want to become. They are moving from an acceptance of the belief structures that they were given as children into a questioning mode. You are there to provide a direction for that questioning, and move them into an "owned faith" at the end of the questions.

These sessions may take more than one week. Not all activities need to be used; pick and choose the ones that fit your group.

Good luck!

Lesson 1
Genesis 1, 2

Creation!

Object: To have students reflect on the beauty of the earth and creation, and to read and discuss the Genesis creation story.

Materials: 3X5 index cards for each person; pencils; model or picture of a scroll; pictures of beautiful things/places in creation, including stars and planets, plants, mountains, weather, etc., displayed around the room if possible; Bibles for each student (preferably modern translations); open minds; sense of humor!

1. Open with "Summer!" 3 x 5 cards — each class member receives a card and a pencil; then answer these questions:
    1) Something GREAT about my summer.
    2) Something LOUSY about my summer.
    3) Something I LEARNED last summer and/or one way I changed.
    4) Not about summer — but something I've CREATED in my lifetime.
   Sign your cards, please! Completed cards are then passed to the teacher. Teacher reads these and everyone tries to guess whose card it is.

2. Discuss plan for the year: The Bible as an open book ...
   Activity: have an imaginary line across the room, as a physical continuum, with one end of the line representing things "easy to understand" and the other end things "almost impossible to understand." Have students get up out of their chairs and stand on the line to represent their feelings about these books or ideas: a first grade storybook; algebra; computer programming; telling time; taking good photographs; building with building blocks; making change; taking a driver's test; college entrance tests; multiplication tables; reading the Bible.

3. Display SCROLLS; discuss origins of Bible as oral tradition, scrolls, etc.

4. Look at universe poster and books of beautiful places; discuss implications, feelings, questions, etc., about creation and things class members said they had created. How did it feel to create something? Do you think God created everything in a literal seven days? What about evolution?

5. Read Genesis 1, 2.

   Discuss differences in story. Talk about Bible as Truth. Look at picture of earth in universe (*National Geographic* poster); discuss Fibonacci series (1, 1, 2, 3, 5, 8, 13, etc.) and other patterns in nature (honeybees' dance as being like quantum physics patterns, etc.) and the intentionality of God as creator!

Note: It's okay for students — and you — to leave this class wondering about God and creation! We certainly don't have all the answers about any of this!

Lesson 2
Genesis 2, 3

Obedience?

Object: To discuss what the concept of obedience is all about, in a personal sense and in the biblical sense, relating it to the Adam and Eve story.

Materials: Copies of this questionnaire, pencils, Bibles

1. Choose a name of a person in your group who is a leader, and play the game "Simon Says" using that person's name. For example: "Joey says, 'Get up.' Joey says, 'Stand on one foot.' Sit down." Only play this for two to five minutes, enough for a few laughs and an opportunity for students to get up and move a little.

2. Talk through the questionnaire on the next page, checking off choices and allowing ample opportunity for discussion. Why do we obey some people and not others? Or if the word "obey" isn't appropriate, why do we do what some people want us to and not others? Do others do what WE ask? Who? Why?

Questionnaire On Obedience

Check all that apply.

1. When my mom asks me to do something, I
   - ❏ ask why first
   - ❏ say "Okay" and then blow it off
   - ❏ obey immediately
   - ❏ do it if I feel like it; depends what it is
   - ❏ ignore her completely
   - ❏ other _____

2. When my dad asks me do something, I
   - ❏ ask why first
   - ❏ say "Okay" and then blow it off
   - ❏ obey immediately
   - ❏ do it if I feel like it; depends what it is
   - ❏ ignore him completely
   - ❏ other _____

3. When my friend (could be girl- or boy- friend if you want) asks me to do something, I
   - ❏ ask why first
   - ❏ say "Okay" and then blow it off
   - ❏ obey immediately
   - ❏ do it if I feel like it; depends what it is
   - ❏ ignore her/him completely
   - ❏ other _____

4. When God asks me to do something (through the "still small voice," a "feeling," through reading the Bible, or hearing a sermon, etc.), I
   - ❏ ask why first
   - ❏ say "Okay" and then blow it off
   - ❏ obey immediately
   - ❏ do it if I feel like it; depends what it is
   - ❏ ignore him completely
   - ❏ other _____

5. Read Genesis 2:16-3:24.
   When God told Adam not to eat the fruit, did Adam
   - ❏ ask why first
   - ❏ say "Okay" and then blow it off
   - ❏ obey immediately
   - ❏ do it if he felt like it; depends what it is
   - ❏ ignore God completely
   - ❏ other _____

6. If you had been Adam (or Eve), how would you have responded to this temptation to know everything and "become as gods"?
   - ❏ I would have obeyed God no matter what
   - ❏ I would like to have the knowledge, but resisted more and been less stupid
   - ❏ I would have done what Adam and Eve did, but argued more about the consequences
   - ❏ I would have done exactly what Adam and Eve did

7. What is your understanding of this passage?
   - ❏ It's a re-hash of *Men Are From Mars, Women Are From Venus*
   - ❏ It shows that women are more easily tempted
   - ❏ It shows that men shouldn't listen to their wives
   - ❏ It shows that people are more likely to disobey God than to obey
   - ❏ It shows that sin has always been a part of who humans are
   - ❏ Other _____

8. Look up Romans 3:23 and/or Romans 5:12. These passages indicate that, given the choice EVERYONE would have made the choice that Adam and Eve did. What do you think?

Lesson 3
Genesis 4

Jealousy, The Green-Eyed Monster

Object: To think about how we may sometimes be jealous, and relate that to the story of Cain and Abel.

Materials: Bibles, pencils, jealousy quiz, a set of postal tags, or cut-out tags that look like those on suitcases at the airport. Put them in a basket for people to draw out for their turn.

1. Have everyone look around the circle, and think of any talent or quality that some person in the room has that you admire, or that you wish you had. Then start the "TAG game." At the end of the game, *everyone* has to have a tag. Teacher starts by giving someone in the room a tag, saying, " If I were you, I would be proud that I ..." That person has to pull out another tag, and give away that tag to someone else with the same words, "If I were you, I would be proud that I ..." or "I really think you are good at ..." until everyone has different tags. This can go on for however long it takes.

2. This was an exercise in the opposite of our real discussion topic, JEALOUSY. It hits everyone! Take this little test and rate yourself.
   Discuss your responses with the group. Do you think the numbers are accurate at the bottom of the scale? If you disagree with them, use your own rating! It's purely arbitrary!

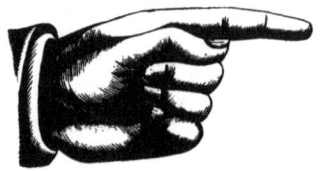

Jealousy Quiz — How do you rate?

Use this scale as points to rate yourself.

10	9	8	7	6	5	4	3	2	1
Definitely!	Pretty often		Sometimes		Kind of		A little	Once	Never!

1. When I see someone who I think looks better than I do,
   I hate him for it. _____

2. When I see someone who gets better grades than I do,
   I despise him for it. _____

3. When I see someone who is a better athlete than I am,
   I can't stand him! _____

4. When I see someone who is more popular than I am,
   I get steamed or depressed. _____

5. I like to cut down people who think that they are "so good"! _____

6. When I feel like my parents think anyone is better than I am,
   including siblings, I see red or feel totally bummed. _____

7. When I see someone driving a better car/motorcycle/truck
   than I'll ever have, I could just scream! _____

8. When my boyfriend or girlfriend starts hanging out or
   flirting with someone else, I just get crazy! _____

9. When I hear that someone else got an honor I think I
   deserved, I feel extremely angry at that person! _____

Total _____

0-25   You're kidding yourself!
26-60 Normal, truly!
61-90 Hmmmm ... can we talk? Stay away from sharp edges!

3. Read Genesis 4:1-17.
   Think about your own jealousies, as you just rated yourself. What are your thoughts about this?
   Was God fair in saying that Abel's offering was better than Cain's?
   Do you think Cain could have kept this murder a secret? For how long?
   Do you think that the punishment was just or unjust? Why?
   What kinds of punishment exist today for murder? Opinions about this?
   What keeps people from being murderers?

4. Read James 1:12-15.
   Are you tempted by God to be jealous?
   Watch out for your imagination about what is happening with someone else — maybe he/she is jealous of you!

Lesson 4
Genesis 5
Through A Flood!

Object: To think about why God might have decided to "flood the earth"; discuss our own thinking about violence; think about what things are valuable; relate these things to the Noah story.

Materials: Bibles

1. Movies/television shows.

    Put an "imaginary line" on the floor, one end being "adore it!" and the other end "abhor it!" or something to that effect. Everyone must line up according to his/her position. They may try to convince others to move if they want to!

    1. car chases
    2. wrestling
    3. nature
    4. football
    5. basketball
    6. science fiction
    7. history
    8. politics
    9. sex
    10. slapstick comedy
    11. shoot-em-ups
    12. things being blown up
    13. cooking
    14. talk shows
    15. cartoons
    16. killing
    17. romance
    18. westerns

2. Going through a flood

    Part a: Decide what you would take with you if you were told your house would be flooded and you might find everything gone — what would you put in your car? You may include possessions, people, pets, anything that will fit in your car!

    Part b: If you had to put one other person in with you, what would you throw out?

3. The Flood — Biblical!

    Read Genesis 5:3-8, 11, 14, 20, 24-27, through Genesis 9 (hit and miss ...)

    Discuss:

    Ages of the patriarchs (Could they really be that old? Why or why not? Can't God do what He wants with folks?)

    VIOLENCE — some translations of Genesis 6:5 cite people's love of violence as being a factor in God's destroying the earth. Remember the choices you made when you made your choices on the line about your interests in violence in television, videos, music ... think about it!

    Are we in for trouble in this country? Why or why not?

Lesson 5
Genesis 12-25
Precious Possessions — What Would You Give Up?

Object: To think about what it meant for Abram to pack up everything and obey God.

Materials: Index cards, pencils, Bibles

1. Game: "Is the price right?" On a card, list your three favorite possessions, and the price that you would ask if you were to sell them. Put your name at the bottom of the card. Every person pass his/her card to the person on the right. Each person will read THE PRICE FIRST, then the group will try to guess what the precious possession is. Discuss: Were many people's the same items? Why were certain things chosen and not others? After hearing what others took, would you change your mind?

2. Abram had to take all his possessions and move, because God gave him a promise. Would the price have been high enough for you to do it? He was 75 when he did this. Read Genesis 12:1-5 and discuss.

3. Reality check. Why would God choose Abraham?
   Why would God choose ANYONE?
   Look up Romans 4:1-5. Now answer: Why did God choose Abraham? Could God choose you for the same reason, or not?

4. Look at some of Abraham's mistakes.
   Genesis 12:11-12; 16:1-4; 17:17; 20:1-4; 22:9-10; 25:5-8
   He was a man whose faith was enough to make him "God's man," but he was obviously capable of making major mistakes and having very human qualities!

5. What things are unforgivable to God? Matthew 12:31-32
   What do you think this means?

6. In what ways are you like Abraham? Why would God chose you?
   Would you say you've done anything unforgivable? Most people might think so, but look at Romans 3:23-24. Soooo?
   In the Old Testament, God spoke to one person at a time (Adam, Cain, Abraham ...) but now, He speaks to all of us! Are you listening?

Lesson 6
Genesis 37-45

Hey, Joe, Nice Coat!

Object: To think about the story of Joseph, his brothers, his suffering, and his ultimate saving of all of Egypt as well as his family during a seven-year famine.

Materials: Index cards, pencils, Bibles, imagination and honesty

1. Yes, another index card! But with a twist. DON'T put your name on this one! Put the letters A, B, C, D, E. Then answer these questions with numbers, 0 being "not me at all — are you kidding?!" and 10 being "YES! This is totally me!"

    A. I lay out my clothes the night before and make sure everything is right.
    B. I have to have name-brand clothes.
    C. I spend more time on looking good than I do on homework.
    D. I often wish I could look like someone on television, movies, or ads.
    E. I think that my parents like some other siblings more than they do me!

    Now, put all the cards in a basket or hat, and pull out one card. Go around the circle and answer the card as if it were you, and give one good excuse for "your" answer! Be creative but not sarcastic!

2. The book of Genesis includes this set of people: Adam, Noah, Abram (later Abraham), Abraham's son Isaac, Isaac's son Jacob (later called Israel), and Jacob's twelve sons (to become the fathers of the "tribes of Israel"). We're skipping up to the story of Jacob's son Joseph. Why? His story starts with clothes: a coat, and the green-eyed monster — JEALOUSY!
    Start reading in Genesis 37:1, through 36. What do you think of Joseph's attitude? How would YOU have felt if you were one of the brothers? Were they justified?

3. Joseph's story picks up again in Genesis 39. Read through it. Now the monster is LUST. Yikes! Should Joe have given in to Potiphar's wife? Why didn't he? Would you have?

4. Continue with Joseph, reading in Genesis 40-41, with his experiences in prison. He correctly interprets the dreams of the baker and the butler. The butler, who lives, says he'll tell Pharaoh about Joseph's amazing powers of interpretation. But when we start Genesis 41, we see that it's been two years! Joseph interprets Pharaoh's dream (look at the end of the chapter) and gets promoted to second in command of the kingdom,

to protect Egypt from the seven-year famine the Pharaoh has dreamed about. Have you had any dreams you felt were warnings, or signs, etc., from God?

5. In Genesis 41, Joseph's family, "back at the ranch" in Canaan, are starving, and hear there is grain in Egypt. They go to Joe, don't recognize him. But he recognizes them and throws them in prison. They do have a conscience (vv. 21-24). What was Joe's reaction? What should he do?

6. Should Joseph have forgiven his brothers? What was his motivation? Look at Chapter 45:1-9. Think about your life — could you be here because GOD BROUGHT YOU HERE?
SELAH ... think about it....

Lesson 7
Exodus 1-9

Holy Moses!

Object: To gain understanding of Moses' calling, his life, and his relationship with God.

Materials: Stopwatch, scratch paper and pencils for notes, Bibles

1. Activity: YOU ARE ON! Think of a topic you feel strongly about: curfews, smoking, social cliques, a certain ref who cheats, licensing guns, drinking and driving, abortion, chewing gum in class, lowering or raising the drinking age, or the driving age. WHATEVER! Then take a few minutes to think up your strongest arguments, because — you will have a full two minutes (and no more!) to state your case. Jot down your thoughts on scratch paper if you want to. Give your argument! Then, with thumbs up or thumbs down, one person (whom the teacher selects) will say, "Yes, you convinced me," or "No, sorry!"
After this activity, talk about how it felt to be "on the spot." Who liked it? Who didn't? Who had the best argument? Would you like that person to speak for you?

2. Exodus picks right up where Genesis leaves off. It was cozy for the Israelites to go to Egypt during Joseph's time, but it got less rosy in a few years. Read Exodus 1:6-15. This is the beginning of the "Moses in the basket" story. He grew up as an Egyptian prince until he killed someone and had to escape. Now — another genuine Bible hero — here is Moses as a murderer and escapee. Why do you think God allows these negative images of His heroes in the Bible?

3. Moses' calling. Exodus 3:1-11. What was Moses' first answer? Why?
Look at Exodus 4:1. What's Moses' second answer? How about 4:10?
Notice God's patience in working with Moses. How does He help Moses feel like the Pharaoh will listen? Would you be able to be persuasive with these tools?

4. Skim through the next few chapters to remind yourself of this story.
Especially note Exodus 9:12. Why was Pharaoh's heart hardened? God did it! Why? How do you think Moses felt about this? Was God being "fair"? Why or why not?

5. Does God still harden hearts today? Consider Jesus talking to his disciples about the religious people of his day in Matthew 13:14-16. What things harden your heart? What things "soften" it?

Lesson 8
Leviticus, Deuteronomy
Laws, Laws, Laws ...

Object: To understand the reason laws were given and to get a brief picture of the types of laws given to the Hebrews.

Materials: Bibles, this question sheet

1. Last time you got to defend something you felt strongly about. Are any of those things laws that you feel should be changed or upheld?

2. What are the "laws" of your household? Whose are strongest, Mom's or Dad's?
    Exodus is the story of how the Israelites got out of Egypt, then went into the desert for forty years. Moses led them until he died, then Joshua led them into the Promised Land. Leviticus, Numbers, and Deuteronomy tell that basic story with the main emphasis on this: LAWS FOR THE ISRAELITES!

3. Let's take a look at some of the laws:
    Offerings to the Lord: Leviticus 1: 1-9. Bloody?
    Peace offering: Leviticus 3:1-5
    Sin offering: Leviticus 4: 13-21
    Notice: for any offering before the Lord, there had to be BLOOD.
    All the surrounding tribes and peoples offered blood sacrifices, but theirs were often human. Those of the Jews NEVER were humans.

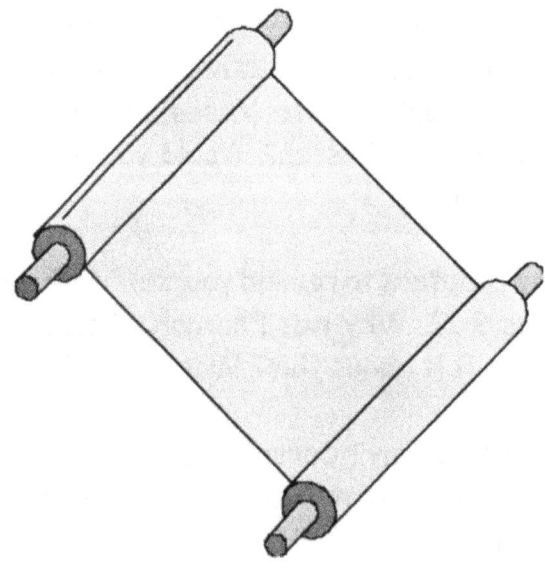

4. Want to become a priest? Watch that thumb and big toe! Leviticus 8:18-24.

5. How about your diet? Leviticus 11. Skim it for your dietary limitations. WHY? Leviticus 11:44-45!

6. Halloween? Hmmm. Leviticus 19:31; 20:6-8, 26-27.

7. What about cursing? Leviticus 24:13-16.

8. What about the well-known blessing that is often used? It was originally Moses' and Aaron's: Numbers 6:22-26.

9. The Ten Commandments: Deuteronomy 5.

10. Here's how you learned them: Deuteronomy 6:4-9.

11. What about virginity? Deuteronomy 22:13-30.

12. Did Jesus come to destroy the Law that the Jews so firmly believed in? Read Luke 16:17 and Matthew 5:17-20.
    How did Jesus "fulfill the Law"?
    Hint: What was the purpose of the Law, anyway?

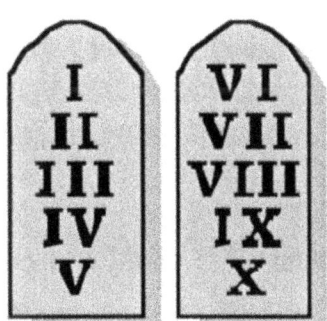

Lesson 9
Joshua

Joshua Fit The Battle Of Jericho, And ...

Object: To compare the taking of Jericho to the taking of Native American lands, and to "judge" how those things were the same and different.

Materials: Table and chairs for the "judges' panel" (each judge could have a big file folder or briefcase, if props are desired); script (below) for participants; Bibles
(*Leaders: Please preread this script and DON'T use it if you don't like it or are offended!*)

Whose Land Is This, Anyway?

Readers: Three judges; Little Star, a Choctaw Indian; Larry Lizard, spokesperson for the United States government; Jehu, a citizen of Jericho; Joshua, leader of the twelve tribes of Israel.

Judge 1: (*Clearing throat*) Uhh-hmm! This panel has convened today in this courtroom to discuss two sets of land grievances. Judge _____, would you please read the first case?

Judge 2: (*Opening his file*) Yes. This panel is authorized to hear the grievances of Little Star, a member of the Choctaw nation.

Judge 3: Speaking on behalf of the United States Government will be Larry Lizard, chairperson of the U.S. Bureau of Indian Affairs.

Judge 1: Thank you. Please go ahead, Mr. (or Ms.) Little Star.

22

Little Star: Yes. On behalf of my tribe, I would like to file a land claim for the city of Atlanta, Georgia.

Judge 2: Excuse me? You must be out of your mind!

Little Star: No, Your Honor. This was land originally held by my people. In the 1830s, the United States Army forcibly moved my people from their homes to what is now Oklahoma. At least a quarter of the thousands who left their homes in Georgia died from hunger, disease, or exhaustion. This was in direct disobedience to the ruling of the Supreme Court at that time, which made a Georgia law depriving native Americans of their rights unconstitutional.

Larry: Excuse me, Your Honors?

Judge 3: Yes, Mr. (Ms.) Lizard.

Larry: In fact, Mr. Andrew Jackson, President at that time, made that decision null and void by signing into law a bill requiring all Indians living east of the Mississippi to leave their homes and be relocated. This bill gave these people thousands of acres of land in which to be reestablished. I believe, in fact, that they have been living happily there ever since. This is a bogus land claim, in my opinion.

Judge 2: That is for this court to decide. We are now ready to hear the other land claim. Mr. Jehu, Mr. Joshua?

Jehu: Yes. My claim is similar to that of Little Star's. The raiding tribes of Israel marched around my city, blowing trumpets. We all thought it was ridiculous, and that we were safe inside our walls. But on the seventh day, BAM! The walls fell down! And their soldiers rushed in and killed everything in sight, except for the family of one traitor, Rahab, the ... uh, "working girl" of the neighborhood. I say that as citizens of Jericho, we have every right to get that land back.

Judge 1: Mr. Joshua?

Joshua: My people and I had been wandering around living in tents for forty years. We had been told by our God to go into this land and take it for our own homeland. Of course, we couldn't leave the inhabitants of that land alive! It was part of our destiny.

Larry: Ah, destiny. That is what made OUR country so great, also.

Little Star: But where is the JUSTICE? What makes one nation so great that it destroys everything in its path?

Jehu: Yes, where is this justice?

Judge 2: Our panel will meet and give you all our decision.

The three judges confer and give their decision. They may choose the spokesperson. A decision must be made in both cases. They should give their reasons for their decision. If they want to have a discussion with the entire class first, that is an option. Good luck!

*****

1. Discuss the similarities of the cases. Read Joshua 1 to get the general idea.

2. What about the claims of each set of people? Should they be taken seriously? What would happen if they were?

3. In a court of law, it may be difficult to prove that God told you to do something. Tradition teaches us that Joshua did, in fact, obey God. He stood ready to do that, even if it meant doing something that seems violent and alien to us today.
   What types of things does God call us to do today?
   Look up Matthew 5, 6, and 7 (The Sermon on the Mount), or 1 Corinthians 13 (the "Love Chapter").

Lesson 10
Judges

Here Come The Judges!

Object: To discuss the biblical "Judges" and the concept of judging.

Materials: Bibles for all; newsprint and markers

1. Activity Continuum: One end of the room is AGREE; the other is DISAGREE. Everyone moves to where he or she "stands" on the continuum. For each statement, people can express verbally why they are standing where they are if they so choose.
   Statements:
   My parents are good judges of my actions: they understand.
   My friends are good judges of my actions: they understand.
   I am the best judge of my own actions: I always know why I make the choices I do.
   I am a good judge of why my friends make the choices they do.
   I think that God is judging me or will judge me at some time.
   I feel comfortable with the thought that God is judging me.

   Today we'll briefly look at the books of Judges and Ruth. In the book of Joshua, many battles were fought so that the Israelites could occupy "The Promised Land" of Canaan. In the book of Judges (and through Kings and Chronicles), the Hebrews are still fighting these battles. They have settled in and around the land, but aren't really organized as a nation. Different people rise up as leaders who sometimes fight against enemies and sometimes judge or rule. The book of Ruth takes place during the same time frame.

2. Activity: Divide into five groups. Read through the passages given, then, using newsprint and markers, come up with information to share with the large group.
   Your task: Create a headline (and first line of an article) about these folks to tell us some of these things: Who, When, Where, What happened, Why, Details. If you would like to make a drawing or cartoon to accompany the headline, DO IT!
   1. Deborah and Barak — Judges 4:1-23
   2. Gideon — Judges 6:33-40 and 7:15-26
   3. Samson — Judges 14:5-19 (Skim also 15)
   4. Samson and Delilah — Judges 16:1-31
   5. Ruth and Naomi — Ruth 1:1-5, 15-22, 4:13-17
   Each group should take time to share their headlines and art, and take questions.

Lesson 11
1 and 2 Samuel, 1 Kings
David, A Man After God's Own Heart — Say WHAT?

Object: To look at King David's life and draw parallels with our own ideas of what it could mean to "be a man or woman after God's own heart."

Materials: Bibles for all; small cut-out red paper hearts, pencils; basket; chart for surveying David's life

1. Activity: Everyone should write on three to five hearts (depending on the size of your group). On each heart they should write their name, and circle it. Then they should write the name of a person, place, thing, or idea which they feel is very much "in their own heart." Put all the hearts back in a basket. Have volunteers come up and draw out a heart, then pantomime what is written there. The group guesses; when they guess right, the volunteer can tell them, and also tell them who wrote the heart. You may have the person who guesses correctly, or other volunteers in the group come up next. Keep the activity going as long as there's interest. Discuss what types of things came up most often, and whether it was difficult or easy to guess who wrote what hearts.

2. The Bible part: Use Bibles and the chart, either as large group, small group, or in pairs, to get a "big picture" of significant events in David's life. If you break into small groups, discuss findings back in large group.

Scripture passage	Event in David's Life	Parallel in my/our lives
1 Samuel 16:1-13		
1 Samuel 17		
1 Samuel 18		
1 Samuel 19		
1 Samuel 24		
2 Samuel 1		
2 Samuel 3:1-12		
2 Samuel 5:17-22		
2 Samuel 6:12-23		
2 Samuel 7:1-6		
2 Samuel 11:1-26		
2 Samuel 12		
2 Samuel 15:1-12		
2 Samuel 18:16-33		
1 Kings 1:1—2:10		

Lesson 12
1 Kings

Power! — The Prophet Elijah

Object: To make students aware of their own personal power, and to get a glimpse of the way God's power worked through Elijah, even when he was feeling alone and sorry for himself.

Materials: Bibles. Read James 5:16-18 and 1 Kings 18-19 (easy-to-read version!).

1. Activity Continuum: One end of the room is ALWAYS; one end is NEVER. Everyone moves to where he or she "stands" on the continuum. Following are the questions to be asked:
    With a lot of people in the car, do you always drive?
    If you're not driving, do you ride shotgun?
    Do you have ways of making parents do what you want?
    Do you control your group of friends? Decisions about where, who, what ...
    Do you control brothers and sisters?
    Are you usually the first ... last person out the door to go somewhere?
    Do people wait for you a lot?
    Do you feel that people in authority listen to your opinion?
    Do you have the remote control 0-100% of the time you're in the room?
    Do you feel God listens to your prayers 0-100% of the time?
    Do you feel that you control your own actions, words, etc.?

2. Discuss power, who has it with friends, family, etc. Why?

3. Read James scripture; discuss power in prayer. ARE we potentially as powerful in prayer as Elijah? If we are, why don't we see it? If we are not, then why not?

4. Read the story of Elijah as readers' theater. To do this, assign readers to be God, Elijah, Angel, and Jezebel, Ahab, and as many Narrators as you want to read in-between texts, and read the passages (1 Kings 18-19, all or parts you select) aloud.
    Discuss power of Elijah, power of the king and queen, power of God.

5. Close in prayer, that each person may be aware of his/her power and aware of the power of God in each life.

Lesson 13
Job

Hey! Ain't No Way That's Fair! What's Up With THIS?

Materials: Bibles for all; note paper and pencils for all

1. Activity: Pass out notepaper and pencils. Have each person in the group write down six of the most important things in his or her life. They may share if you want to. Then the leader asks each person to choose one thing to tear off the paper — to "get rid of." Talk about these choices. Next, the leader walks around and randomly tears off one or two more from each person's list. Discuss how this feels; how people feel when circumstances take away things that are most precious to them. Discuss: Is it ever GOD who does the taking? Why?

    We're looking at the book of Job today. In most of the rest of the Old Testament, the rule is: obey God and the commandments, and you'll be blessed. Disobey, and you'll be cursed. In Job, which some scholars say was originally a play of sorts, this is not the case. Why does God act the way He does? The only answer we're given, in the book itself, is that God is God; no one was there when He called creation into being and we'll never understand. It's okay not to have all the answers as the leader — no one does!

2. Have volunteers read these passages, and discuss:
    What Job was like; what his life was like; how God is pictured; why God does this to Job; how the story is resolved.
    What happened? Job 1, 2 and 3:1:
    Job's friends' comments: Eliphaz — Job 5:17-19; Bildad — Job 8:6. These felt Job must have sinned; Zophar — Job 11:14-17
    Job's answer: Job 13:1-6; 24:16-17; He maintains innocence and grief. Elihu — Job 31:3; 37:14-15 — "Give up, Job"
    God's answer: Job 38, 39, 40 (read portions of these): "Look at all I have created: how dare you question me?"
    Job answers God: Job 42:1-6
    God deals with Job's friends who had wrongfully accused him of being a sinner: Job 42:7-8
    God restores Job's fortunes: Job 42:9 ff. (Note: this last chapter is a later text than the original book; scholars say that it may have been added by ancient redactors who wanted a "happy ending.")

Note: This activity was introduced to me by a hospice worker, Kathy Rittenhouse, who was talking to my third grade class about loss, grief, and death.

Lesson 14
Psalms, Proverbs, Ecclesiastes, Song of Solomon
How Are You Feeling?

Object: to acquaint readers with the amazing range of emotions expressed by the writers of these books.

Materials: Bibles; large sheet of newsprint; access to this list; notepaper and pencils (Optional: quiet "thinking" music)

1. Have people close their eyes for just a few minutes and mentally walk through the past week. You can have some soft music playing if you want. Then have them write down NOT EVENTS but as many feelings or emotions as they can remember having during the week.

2. Have volunteers pantomime some of these emotions and see if the group can guess them. Do this for five to ten minutes as long as there's interest.

3. Brainstorm: let one person write down on the newsprint as many emotions as the group can throw out. Then pass out Bibles and list of applicable scriptures. Discuss the fact that some of the Psalms were written by David, who was said to have been "a man after God's own heart," because although he was an admittedly sinful person, he was very repentant and always tried to do what he felt God wanted. Proverbs and Ecclesiastes are collections of wisdom for living. Song of Songs may be read as a love poem or as an allegory of Christ and the Church.

4. Have group members look up passages and read them for appropriate emotions.

5. Encourage class members to keep these lists and add to them, and to read these passages at home in private, and to think about them and perhaps memorize the ones that are most helpful.

Note to teachers: Here is a case where some students will be very affected in a positive way by the words of the scriptures, and others will be bored. Don't be discouraged! Remember that, even for you, some scripture passages speak to you at one time, some at another, depending on everything from your stress levels to what you ate for breakfast or the fight you had with family members this morning getting ready to come to church! Pray for the Holy Spirit to open the hearts of your class members, so that they will hear God's voice speaking to them through these writings. This is just a quick trip through these books, but they can be very powerful resources in the life a committed Christian!

Emotion or Feeling	Where to look
Everyone is against you	Psalm 3:1-6; 6:6-10; 25:1-3; 35:22-27; 57:6-10; 69:1-3, 13-17
unable or afraid to sleep	Psalm 4:8; 63:5-8; 121:1-8; 127:1-2; 131:1-6
feeling poor or broke	Psalm 9:17; 37:25-26; 41:1-4; 72:12-14; 107:4-9; 113:5-8
feeling stressed, overwhelmed	Psalm 127:1-2; Proverbs 16:3 Ecclesiastes 2:9-12; 2:24-26; 11:9-10
tempted to lie or gossip	Psalm 15:1-4; 141:3; Proverbs 20:19; Ecclesiastes 5:2
joyful	Psalm 16:11; 103:1-5; 104:33-34; 126:1-3; 150
fearful of others hurting you	Psalm 17:6-15; 27:1-3, 5; 56:4-11
unsure of God's power to help you	Psalm 18:6-19; 20:7; 30:4-5; 36:5-9; 118:5-9; 121:1-8; 125:1-2; 136:3; 147:1-6
unsure of God's presence in your life	Psalm 103:1-8; 143:7-8
depressed or ill	Psalm 22:6-11, 14-24; 31:9-15; 40:11-17; 45:14, 18 69:1-3, 13-17; 77:1-18; 102:1-11, 28; 103:1-3
needing comfort	Psalm 23:1-6; 36:5-9; 61:1-4; 91:1-4; 103:8-14; 121:1-8
guilty	Psalm 25:6-18; 32:1-5; 48:1-22; 51:1-12; 130:1-6; 145:8-9
weepy, crying a lot	Psalm 40:5b; 31:99-16; 42:1-11; 56:8; 62:8; 69:1-3, 13-17; 86:1-7; 126:5-6; Ecclesiastes 3:1-8
worried	Psalm 32:6-7; 103:8-14
tempted	Psalm 119:1-3, 9, 93, 105; 120:1-2; Proverbs 22:1

Emotion or Feeling	Where to look
shy; afraid	Psalm 10:17-18; 12:5; 55:4-8
can't find God	Psalm 13:1-6; 31:21-24; 69:13-18; 77:1-18; 139:1-18
wondering about God's power	Psalm 19:1-6; 24:1-2; 29; 33:6-7; 46:1-3; 53:2-5; 65:5-13; 97:1-6; 99:1-3; 104:1-30; 145:1-8
lazy	Proverbs 6:6-11; 10:4; 10:26
bored	Ecclesiastes 1:2-10
fearful of disasters	Psalm 46:1-3; 50:15; 55:4-11; 57:1-2; 91:1-16; 107:25-31; Proverbs 25-26
hopeless	Psalm 6:5; 62:5-7
in love — head over heels?	Song of Solomon (Song of Songs) 8:6-7
brokenhearted	Psalm 34:18; 17; 55:22; 61:1-4
feeling like you can't get what you want	Psalm 37:3-4

Lesson 15
Prophets

Okay, NOW You're In Trouble!

Object: To introduce students to some of the prophets, their calling, their purpose.

Materials: Chalkboard or newsprint; Bibles for all; cut-up magazine and/or newspaper headlines about injustice, cruelty, violence, natural disasters; index cards and pencils for all; megaphone or toy hand microphone. Copy the page with scripture blocks* (page 35) and cut up the names and scriptures to give to volunteers.

1. Play this clapping game as a warm-up. People position their hands ready to clap. You say, "This is an ancient game that was used to train warriors to be ready and responsive to anything. Watch me — clap only when I clap. Ready —" Then clap, encouraging, smiling, etc. then — QUIT! Do this and tell them that you're trying to trick them. Encourage laughing and having fun. Try to really trick them by random clapping! Keep this going for two to four minutes.*

2. On chalkboard or newsprint, write the words: JUSTICE, REPENTANCE, VENGEANCE, MERCY. Pass out the headlines and have people read them and discuss them in relation to these four words. Discuss how reading about these things makes them feel about God.

3. Pass out index cards and pencils. Ask them to put their names at the top, then write down three things that they feel are "wrong with the world today." Collect these. Leader or volunteer can read each one and have the class guess who wrote each. Hearing each others' ideas can spark others.

4. Get out the megaphone (if you don't have one, roll up a piece of paper for dramatic effect!) and ask for volunteers to come up and speak to the group about how each person there could change personally to affect some of these "wrongs." Encourage emotional, strong appeals, even like old-time preaching, "repent or go to hell," "wrath is coming," or campaigning.

5. Pass out Bibles and the cut-up last page (page 35) to volunteer readers. Discuss God's calling of the prophets. Theirs was not an easy life. In fact, God told Ezekiel that if he didn't warn the people as God told him to, he would be punished as they were! Have everyone turn to the scripture passages. Listen to and discuss these prophets, and talk about whether any of their messages are valid today and why.

6. Close in prayer for each other, the nation, and the world.

_____

*Created by Birgitta DePree, professional actor, and used with permission.

Isaiah
Isaiah's purpose was to call back Judah to God and to prophecy about the salvation of God through the Messiah.
Judgment: Isaiah 1:14-20
Isaiah's calling: Isaiah 6:1-13
Prophecy of Christ: Isaiah 9:2-6; 11:1-3
Comfort: Isaiah 12:2-3; 43:1-3; 55:12

Jeremiah
Jeremiah's purpose was to turn people back from their sins to God.
Jeremiah's calling: Jeremiah 1:4-10
Judgment: Jeremiah 5:1-9
Destruction: Lamentations 2:19-22
Comfort: Jeremiah 3:15; Lamentations 3:22-23

Ezekiel
Ezekiel's purpose was to turn people back from their sins to God.
Ezekiel's calling: Ezekiel 1; 3:18-19
Judgment: Ezekiel 7
The mark of the Lord: Ezekiel 9
Cherubim: Ezekiel 10

Daniel
Daniel's purpose was to stay true to God as an exile in a foreign land.
His exile: Daniel 1
Interprets dream: Daniel 2, 4
Fiery furnace: Daniel 3
Lions: Daniel 6
Visions of end times: Daniel 7

Jonah
Jonah was called by God to prophecy to Ninevah but Jonah didn't want to!
Jonah's calling, refusal, big fish: Jonah 1
Ninevah repents and Jonah pouts: Jonah 2-4

"Minor" prophets (short books of prophecy): Micah, Nahum, Habbakuk, Zephaniah, Haggai, Zechariah, Malachi
Purpose: To warn people to turn back to God or they would be killed, exiled, etc.
Also prophecies of coming Savior.
Key verse: Micah 6:8

www.ingramcontent.com/pod-product-compliance
Lightning Source LLC
Chambersburg PA
CBHW081351040426
42450CB00015B/3402